Time Beginnings

Time Beginnings

POEMS

James Applewhite

Louisiana State University Press

Baton Rouge

Published by Louisiana State University Press
Copyright © 2017 by James Applewhite
All rights reserved
Manufactured in the United States of America
LSU Press Paperback Original
First printing

Designer: Laura Roubique Gleason
Typefaces: Whitman, text; Filosofia, display
Printer and binder: LSI

Library of Congress Cataloging-in-Publication Data

Names: Applewhite, James, author.
Title: Time beginnings : poems / James Applewhite.
Description: Baton Rouge : Louisiana State University Press, 2017.
Identifiers: LCCN 2017036580 | ISBN 978-0-8071-6687-1 (pbk. : alk.
    paper) | ISBN 978-0-8071-6688-8 (pdf) | ISBN 978-0-8071-6689-5
    (epub)
Classification: LCC PS3551.P67 A6 2017 | DDC 811/.54—dc23
LC record available at https://lccn.loc.gov/2017036580

"Rilke in the Mountains" and "A Walk in the Park" were published
previously in the Hudson Review. "Among the Empiricists," "A Dream of
the Sun," "Dreaming England," "The Lost Child," "Steps Up the Steep
Bank," "The Serpent," and "Thinking with Clouds" were published
previously in the North Carolina Literary Review. "Strange Sleep" was
published previously in One.

Contents

Time Beginnings

Thinking with Clouds

I

Clouds last evening looked swollen with rain
but turned golden at sundown, illuminating
distances. Then violets and diaphanously
purpling layers built up haunting presences—
airy, empathic entities of radiance
and gloom. Night darkened at the edges we
were driving into as horizons receded.
Dream-beings permitted a consciousness
in time, we raced on toward the mysteries
we couldn't explain, at a speed to end
us quite, if we encountered the vehicle
of some other person's strange knowing.

Our self-definition today takes shape
from our treeshaded room's Palladian windows.
Why this barrier between us and everything else?
Here bookcases line the walls yet
illumination comes in from outside—
cloud shadows impinging upon us,
alternating radiance and gloom—
our moods as ephemeral as the weather's.

II

My wife is polishing the granite countertops
and I hear water gurgling the drain—like
the leaking away of all we see and say.
Yet the mind's magic castle suspends itself
between sky and earth, our shared and different
consciousnesses swept between sun and rain.

And so she works on her tapestry,
while writing orders my *ideas,* this moment—
these ill-defined unions half-present in words,
that now seem sliding from my head and
along my arm and hand and onto
the paper. What a frail center—like
a page as it is whirled in the vortex
of a tornado, that in its dynamic
of near and far, of now and then,
of me and everything else is trying
to tell me who and what I am, presently.

III

Here in the swift-floating years
we reflect on the clouds. Our singular
view among unfettered horizons
darkens at the edges, recalling those
dream-like towers we saw last night—
as if taking us along on their jaunt
across darkness and light.

Cosmologists Hiking at Sunset

Our shadows lengthen at sunset
cast behind us by a leveling light—
as if struggling against a resistant medium
that is measuring our effort in crossing it—
we figures stilled in the frieze of time.

Strange Sleep

War refugees, we totter about
the proving grounds, fitting
brass rings into retainers—
the sand a problem—recognizing
each other by gestures
recalling our surviving
lab fires, explosions—
our selfhoods diminished
in this desert now used for
movies about apocalypse—
we child-sized ones still
finding each other
in our roles as civilians—
swept up in extremity,
shrunk to half our heights
by this sky holding hands as
we look at each other with
the exquisite longing
of old lovers reunited
though our history of passion
drifts away toward morning
when on into waking I
cannot find identities
only feeling without body
what it once must have meant
just to wish and have it
granted in knowing life.

Alone on the Holiday Campus

The airliner arrows
      an urgent aspiration
            its idea elsewhere
                  my slow walk a circuit.

A winterward willow-oak
      engraves the silvering air
            with infinite particularity
                  its stasis like motion.

Bound into a diurnal round
      I pass with gifts and regrets—
            many students, colleagues, flights
                  that poetry still brightens

my mindscape this horizon
      a calligraphy, a history, my heights
            and depths, the regrets not
                  paramount, the mind's delights

I helped ignite around me like
      stars discerned in a day that's
not yet ready to dim, not quite
                  while these winter trees ink light.

Afterward

Through Eden took their solitary way.

I

That day in Eden waking
merely breathing opened their feeling
as into a song. They dallied along
twin rivers, that meandered among
the islands of flowers. Without ever
moving from sun to shower, currents
swept their reflections past
each taste of happiness. Repasts
of fruits and flowers would follow
their kisses, each one a swallow
of fragrance within the embraces.
Their ideas as a flowing stasis
and vision as if everywhere conscious
held the garden whole within them,
as one moment's color became another.

II

Eve watched the rippling river
still within its faceted shimmer.
As she followed the winding water,
she saw a mark on the bank—
the moving S of a snake.
It traveled the rocks, like a thought
against Adam's father.
She ate the delicious fruit
from a tree that fed her anger.

III

"He says these scenes are forever,"
she mused. "Yet I feel this current
like something not conjured yet.
As I wade, it touches my marrow.
I dream a tomorrow,
when Adam comes to me—
not bringing fruit but inside me
somehow. Flowing is like a sorrow
but creates difference
between each quick day, the chance
of a cloud, its shade across a pool.
Shadow after sun feels cool,
and blossoming changes, even in spring."

IV

She disclosed these things to Adam,
who held her differently. This love
alive between them would shatter
their figures reflected on water.
A wind-like feeling springing
again and again let beginning
move on toward ending.
Aware of the moments of passion
their minds now felt division.
With Adam, happily forlorn,
Eve knew of emotions, born
of longing—and of dreams
like leaves in coming autumns.

V

At evening, chilled and bare
she saw a shooting star—
then the moon's new phase.
Half-glimpsing ways to come
she foresaw a branching maze—
like a tree that misled them.
Aware of bruises and fatigued
she faced the sinking sun,
then turned toward Adam.

Events

Provisionally we accept
the randomness of events—
our thoughts quick-lit
by dove flight
above an accident—

by thought of if and whether—
we unable to foresee
the small, immense
distance
in pulling a trigger.

The lightning flashing
precedes our being aware
the thunder later
like a mind turning over
its reasons, decisions.

In the wee hours—
the paper on the drive—
sleepless, we go out
on the gravel and pick up
a plastic wrapper full
of the sorrows of others.

Each grief like
a grain of sand
comes in through
the lips of shell
to be told into pearl
by the hurt that
holds it.

Each accident
each death by chance
brings sufferings,
in guises
we cannot have
imagined
and recognize.

The Lost Child

The lost child returned to her alone
materializing among the walking figures
from sun at the horizon on sand by the ocean
cloaked in mist like the mystery of years.

Time had given this infant, nails perfect
on doll-sized fingers her lashes delicately
outlining the eyelids she growing like the subject
of a novel, talking so early then lightly

running over the lawn. One day she was gone
from her grandmother's—alone downtown
in the safe southern hamlet while on
to her grandfather's store—not to this bourn

between her living presence and a persistence
in memory, ever as if just around a corner
only chance deferring a promised reappearance
in the hurt hope haunting the heart of her mother.

Her mother peered into the haze as if to pierce
the lost years. She searched those faces defining
themselves above waists and shoulders her fierce
desire of love hovering brows imagining

in rending detail how her daughter
would surely look now each older feature
exact in her mind's eye part of a figure
she would recognize—though like many another.

But then her mother reasoned even if *she*
may have so changed still *her* eyes
will see me as I was. But hazed by the sea
what if she returned an unrecognizing gaze?

The mother scrutinized those girls, similar in difference
as they magnified themselves each step the reunion
she so long had sought dissolving into resemblance—
this lovely young human not her longed-for *one*—

so that she had to turn aside her tears
from this leggy thirteen-year-old whose chance
for good luck along the perspective of years
remained. Her child walked still in remembrance.

To Think of It All

The nebula-idea infiltrates consciousness
an exquisite adjustment of constants
my matrix, an intelligence-parallax
flashing from quasars like lighthouses,
measuring out immensity in its *becoming*.
Later stars burn down to iron then
supernova violences synthesize heavier
elements, dispersing them into spaces
for smaller more complex stars—these
long-lived points in distances so vast
that the time of a travel between them
means manyness created from a one.

A galaxy stabilizes in its three dimensions
inheriting the star-dust elements, subsiding
into its spiral locality, energy-as-matter
re-igniting, gravity crushing it to fusion.
Centered on a hungry black hole, this disc
inherits the element-ashes of aboriginal
explosions and collapses. Then one cooler
system in the galactic periphery
creates a planet in its mid-range orbit
steadied about a long-lived star.
Having survived its aggregation by
asteroid bombardment, then rocky huge
snowballs raining in, it collides with
a planet almost half its size, that
knocks its axis of rotation twenty-
three-and-a-half degrees away from
perpendicular to its orbital plane
so that later there will be seasons.

Now the silicate residue ejected into
orbit by the fiery impact re-condenses
into a sphere, leaving this Earth stabilized
in a circuit of its mid-sized star by one
large moon. The ashes of billions of years
of star-births, burnings, supernova explosions
have collected in this cosmic miniature—
a planet tiny in the spaces toward infinity
comprising in itself all the synthesized
elements. And iron, last to be created
in the regular sequence of star burning
has abundantly centered this rocky sphere—
the dynamo effect of its molten interior
creating electromagnetic force-fields
about it, protecting the nascent atmosphere
with vectors arising and descending at
the poles, deflecting the charged particles
from storms on the star its sun.
An increasingly complex chemistry has
arisen on shores of its unfrozen oceans—
a molecular transcription wherein the new
process records its history, and builds on
this, through random variations selected
by survival. A long evolution unfolds.
Creatures reflecting the violent simplicity
of these explosions into being aggregate
in a shoreline foam, cell-walls toughened
from the surface tensions, as from first bubbles
in the slime—then larger cells ingesting
the smaller, the momentous division
into multicellular being, the self-replications
succeeding themselves more rapidly, flagella
propelling elongated creatures along the one-

way arrow of time, inventing narrative—
the beginning middle and end. Jaws arise
pushed through the fluid changes by flexing
sinuous bodies, in vectors of life-competition.
Seas as invisible to these as the fluid
of time surround this wriggling of each
toward self-replication, individual extinction.
The nerve-cord node with eye spots
allows a first awareness, the quick glance
before and after, foretelling a consciousness
of self, the life lived knowing of death.
Though nothing can bring back the hour
and white light of first existence
yet the backward glances accumulate,
write their divisions into life's precedent.

This transmitting of the self-transcription
accelerates changes, the code grows
richer, so that we selected variants
here see mathematically rearward toward
the infinite-seeming origin of all stars.

Aware of this improbable series of events
toward consciousness, our species
ponders the fragmented scintillant bits
of coherence and chance, in an energy-
origin that aligned this brain toward
eventually seeing its start: thermodynamics
of the energy-arrow, that we now discern—
in a residual origin-hum, here lately
still echoing from the dawn of time.
Belatedly, our species computes events
in the sequence of our coming hence—

the coherences requisite in a first violence.
Our mind in its brain with the billions
of neurons and the trillions of dendritic
connections finds an improbability
resembling the old term *miracle*.
We know with a glow in the mind
to which the stars correspond. We're
given these years to ponder our arisal—
for conceiving star-birth in first dark—
then the exacting burnings seeding intelligence
in its mirroring of a begetting light.

Steps Up the Steep Bank

Sight by the light of tonight's half-
risen moon thump-stops my heart
this moment. *I* is not important.
The howl of a prowling owl
whets my knife in its sheath. A pull
of this wild is crushing my height
pulling me prone on the flank of
a ridge as high as a house above me.
Again I've carved new trail into this
bank of rock and earth and root—
nailing-in cedar steps with spikes
I've cut also from the dead unrotting trunks.
While light is not quite gone
I climb again into view of those
far yellow windows. Here I
am at home in night. Under no
uniting light of sun or moon
each tree's gnarled reach seems
seeking a single different star
it grows toward—and cannot touch.

Here I am awake for a while
as the horizon moves to disclose
those stars it has buried deeper, if
only because the Earth's wide curve
has hidden them earlier. I feel
beyond its bound, as it turns
into its own great shadow, enlarging
all that I see by daylight—
the roads and houses. Owls call
and a farther night seems home.

Let the deeper sleep come on
whenever it will. I am
a creature of this night.
Daylight blinds me.

Now in semi-dark I see
as this steel hammer in
my hand drives the cedar
sharpened wood into the rocks
and soil and writes me human
in this universe of fact and wish
wherein I perish through these
fictional years but flourish
out here for a time—whatever
time is—perched on a slope
where if I make a slight
mistake I will roll and fall
into the current below me and
not so much be lost I think
because here on the slope in
coming night I know I am
alive. Time is unreal under
a sidereal movement apparent
from Earth's spinning ball—
my address in the cosmos.

Rilke in the Mountains

Randall Jarrell reads his just
translated "The Great Night"
hanging before us, I the new
instructor among a handful of students
that Greensboro so long ago it seems
also a poem inside a dream.
Then with his image beside me I
climb the suspending slope of our
cottage, Randall's slight presence
whispering of the land become pink
light near sunset. This slant
across wild asters and thistles
takes in the blackberry roughness
and purples the substance of a granite
rooting as if into the evanescence
of time and thought. Only then
I notice on our right the stones
of graves from the church in the valley.
The chiseled identities cut the tissued
brightnesses connecting our breathing
on into a westward horizon. I remember
his syllables falling musically precisely,
conveying us into a different country
in a century also only a part of history.

Reflections on a Mountain Lake

For Jan

I

The lake as nearly perfect circle
holds sun and shadow, slick and ripple,
reflecting clouds like imagination.

A wind's quick touch, like iteration
of years beyond a far horizon
arouses thoughts of things ideal.

My dreams of early life create
a meadow with a brighter sun
where the real and the seeming in debate

depict me as I'm beckoned on
by a little girl in shining vapor,
where hills, as in two facing mirrors

suspend between the past and future
this path I walk toward her *forever*—
unable to choose a living lover.

II

She plays in roses by a castle ruin.
The bud I pick and offer her
bloodies her finger and she is gone—

vanished into a morning aether
where real/unreal are ever either
and hills on hills recede forever.

Her absence through a seeming error
held me still as within a mirror
where real/ideal were ever either—

distorting time in a life among
wife and children, carrying on
a dream-beginning, as if at dawn

I'd fall from this more perfect world—
a child-beloved there preferred.
Injured by these ideals of dream

I had no real world art-recourse—
depicting still this timeless scene
that thinned away my given voice.

Then nature became my surrogate—
replacing the beauties only met
in sleep's deceptive, haunted mirror.

III

Now sky as if an ideal other
inverted here in mountain water
shines below the surface shimmer.

This mirroring by a smoother lake
alters, as when a breeze's wake
roughens the scene it will reflect.

Then two swans settle on the pond
and paddle together, around, around
having just come down from the wind.

They venture into deeper shadow
where trees inverted within water
seem love-illusions seasons earlier—

when life obscured by an ideal
distorted the sunny love I'd feel
in meadows of the passing real.

This present pair upon the pond
here paddle together, all around
as if just appeared from the mind.

In feathered brilliance, sunny white
upon this surface, defining light
they trail behind their every movement

interlocking, perfect circles.
Now we invoke love's pastoral
as shining moments we two feel—

in chains of instants, that endure
like past and future, seen from shore
in our reflections this September.

Among the Empiricists

Vivid in the atmosphere down through a pine
light defines this yellow-brown autumn.
The mind I'm taught thinks in data-equivalents
the web of its sight strung on wave-like points
whereby stars strike into my eyes
as these ends of rays—their lines of flight
through a space-as-time that light years
calculate. Without me or someone nothing appears
of this pointillist brilliance—
this visual condensation of distance
in a universe that's origin of consciousness.

By the dispersal of star-fused elements
we know ourselves the descendants
of a big bang into existence: first point
for our travel on an evolution into the light.
It persists, an illumination within, a sense
that consoles this declining, as a brightness
from our near star lets us nightly go hence
into Earth-cast shadow. Then rays of starlight
touch again into sight each a dot
as I see it—an angle infinitely acute
image of a fiery ball unimaginably distant.
When such light years pierce my sight, I say
quietly the old word "eternity."

Poet Briefly in Office

Durham, by the Eno River

A runner I bisected the currents
hand over hand along high-strung cables
aware of the river, tense within determinants
as in two lines from a musical clef.
The tight steel held me truly myself
breathing in a rhythm of syllables
crossing these arcs of earth-surface
within orders emerging from chaos.
I suspended myself in moments
over river-rush swirling like serpents
under power lines in stationary movement
among tensions I was born to reflect.
I ran the far bank and returned
the script I wrote to remember
only sweat-stained ink upon paper.

Currents of sensation trailed the page
among thoughts running through me in language.
Running where others would walk
I sometimes stopped with a laugh
immobile on the twisting path
alerted by a subliminal glance
at a crook not a root but a snake.

By friends made Director of the Arts
I felt myself random in events—
freeing Dance from Physical Ed
seeing artistry in ordinary history
running rhymes within rhythms in my head.
I imagined a poetry of physics

in these moving bodies' aesthetics
when dancers inscribed a suave surface
in an orderly-chaotic sequence.
Organizing dances and concerts
within tensioned steel-like determinants
I myself danced upon chaos—
the clef of my wayward musics
notated by the laws of physics,
and by cautionary conferences with the Dean
for whom art must academically *mean*.
While dancers in imaginary heights
rehearsed among my riverside sights
I mirrored these movements
in a consciousness of river currents.

Moving on in the course of events
I wondered how I'd spent so long
loving poetry painting dance and song
ever in midair when writing my form
not strictly proper an order too random.
I sometimes cross by wire
over the continuing currents in metaphor
dancing along new balances
in this riverside life-by-chance.

Astronomer by the River

The natural world may be
conceived of as a system of
concentric circles . . . which
apprize us that this surface
on which we now stand is not
fixed, but sliding.
        —Emerson, *Circles*

A broken, time-bent hickory leaned
above the windless river-surface.
Rings appeared for no visible cause
as in my old refractor, out of focus
expanding far stars into aureoles.
Descending the rocky bank, I saw no
minnows underneath. I gave the trunk
a shake and saw a magic increase—
this air so heavily wet, that drops
condensed on the withered leaves and fell.
Trees shone inverted from the opposite
shore, reflected there as if down below—
like an irregular world to come from
a beginning in this perfect geometry.

The roundnesses propagated swiftly,
wrinkling the surface tension, marking
as surely as a draftsman's compass
these single designs in water, circles
within circles, concentrically outward
each impulse from a falling drop
traveling along its line of time
but there all together, a bending perimeter,
a figure without beginning and ending—
a geometry on the river by chance
within symmetries before the birth of the stars.

Dinner at Twilight

Our faces brightened as a pink light
irradiated the window. Scrolls of cerise
unrolled, a goldenness bulged up from below
long diaphanous rays shot out
from the sun behind a granite horizon.
An Edenic orient hovered the horizontally
layered purples we looking out across
the restaurant parking lot with its cars
toward the one bare tree. We sat side by side
in the booth while time was suspended.
Until it faded. I returned to my seat
facing you. Your expression grew weary.
I recognized the thoughts you were thinking.
Then a flicker of last pink lit your cheek
with the innocence of an Eve our meal
uneaten part of a future yet before us
in a sunset over the mountain.

A Dream of the Sun

When I awaken from the dream
returning to space and time
from an orbit above the sun
I come to myself alone as I am spun
about a center of half-molten iron.
The sun's seeming rise makes appear
the beginning of a day, of a year.
Centered again in seeing I can peer
all about where faces and flowers wear
their colors and then pass into night.
I see the sun's rise and sun's set
separate the dark from the light.
As Earth is center for the moon
so is Earth held in orbit by the sun.
I felt lonely and far gone
there in sleep but awake I am borne
within appearances of far and near
as I travel in the circuit of a year.
Roads mark days into a line
but remembering the dream I return
to the cycling of seasons like a rhyme
within the strange circumferences of time.
As the sun created light and our eyes
so the years and hours
mark measures that are also ours.
These spaces hold our mind's realizing
of the meaning of our star in its shining.

But the idea of our yearly orbit
as circular regular and perfect
is a course the Earth cannot run
as it spins while going around the sun.

In these ellipses of time
on an Earth that is familiar as my home
my soul dreams a farther circle
as it figures the greater whole.
From the region of my consciousness
I yearn and turn toward a source
even farther than the sun:
beyond time's separation into a line
and this reasoning in seasons.
Then Earth's orbit bends in turning
toward an end in its beginning.

Science Fictions: A Sequence

> . . . our brains interpret the input from our sensory organs by
> making a model of the outside world.
> —Stephen Hawking

Prehistory

First darkness sharp with points of light
in space they had not named as night
by moving promised shapes of thought.
Through long times evolving on planet Earth
they hunted and gathered the plains of birth
aspiring in glory through mountain pass
in icy heightenings of consciousness—
their first ideas these likenesses.
Their minds roamed with the animal droves
they painted stilled on walls of caves.
Defining themselves with ornament
they gestured in sounds that newly *meant*.
They praised and mourned with measured breath
deft fingers wove their fleece as cloth
to shroud those lost in frost of death.
They found and made new tribal bounds
dreaming of kingdoms without ends.
They founded history in honored place
upon Earth's violent, altering surface.

Monuments and Marriages

The hills and fields of victories
framed monuments with broken trees
where stones that marked the bodies mourned
and bound within time's bourne were turned

in soil of Earth's diurnal round.
Earth measured days with sunset ending
always the seasons' orbits bending
toward dawns like a renewed beginning—
like spring returning after winter
that birds in mating celebrate, as clouds appear
in resurrectional darknesses. Branches bare
as though in death renewed the year
when blossoming. Larks taught to sing
by winds through meadows whistling
the pear tree and the pine
chorused of life's decline-return.
Each boy's and girl's acutest feeling
mirrored the other's eyes in union
celebrated as ritual wedding
achieved by blood of men and women.
In communal dancing round a maypole
man and woman became a couple—
so fields and seasons spun and bound
these two as centering hallowed ground—
each finding the other's bodily grace
an offspring-promise in sacred space.
Each season's returning bade her wear
blossoming apple twigs twining hair.

The people lived in righteousness, though
others abused these mysteries so
that peasants bound in humble awe
to sacrifices and eternities
with sighing praise of weary breath
bowed low in those laborious days
of building soaring aisle and vault
that echoed ancient pieties

promising only after death
the heavenly Earth they glimpsed and sought.

Herdsmen

Smoke rose from lowly cottages
in shapes like peasant miseries
wreathing the fields around the valleys
that dimmed beneath the twilight heavens.
Stars moved above the kitchen gardens
and churches' graves inscribed with names.
They walked their vales within the frames
of craggy local eminences, while lakes
and flumes refreshed demesnes
where evening vapors for their sakes
veiled human life in somber drapes
that closed upon their final scenes.
Maternal elms bent-limbed through years
hemmed in these places known through tears
as *home* beneath the icy stars.
No knowledge raised their minds beyond
their paths to pasture and watering pond
and the patient herd that stood like them
bemused within the dream of time.

Sciences Fictions

These skies these fields these cloud-like trees
these crystalline azure distances
depend upon the verities
of quarks and speeds and quantities
whereby blood flows and vision sees.
Within the certain uncertainties

that balance kinetic energy's
centrifugal force with gravity's
holding round the air one breathes,
we orbit in the brilliances
of near-star day, night galaxies.

Rounding in seasonal slight ellipses
the Earth brings dream-like imageries
Late autumn sun's pink-oranges
blaze the horizon like elegies.
Flowers color our languages.
Our body's complex surfaces
pang their acute imperatives,
while cemeteries and nurseries
define the final boundaries.
Encoded sensory languages
quicken breaths like eternities
when conjugating the he's and she's.

We exist by arcane symmetries
old movies' unreal realities
as unlikely as these centuries
of science religion philosophies
warfare ruin false pieties
why primates came to plains from trees.
My dreams become like reveries
synopses of the reels of days.

Earth Minds in Space

Creation's spacetime universe
evolved myself and consciousness—
the *self* and *other* an obvious

problem in energy's spaciousness.
Our nervous system's correspondence
to quantum state and random dance
still beams a dream world into us,
that to me feels strangely precious.

Mind knows itself in evanescence
briefly thinking of permanence
creating within its consciousness
displays of mice and galaxies.
One feels and sees almost believes
that birth and death are elegies
and clouds and trees their languages—
we enticed by color preferences
evolved among the flowers and bees.

Imagining Origin

Dreaming distant bits of light
I think before this starry night
to spacetime spreading from a point—
yet can't imagine original vacuum,
conscious only in after-time.
And yet. And yet. I guess through hints
in thoughts *before* that rain as glints
like cosmic rays through consciousness—
the shapes of things I would express
mere sparks within the randomness.
Thinking beginnings before time
exploring space from here indoors
I sense the distance years have come
from stars down lonely corridors.

Sacred Visions

If a universe in violence
exploded from a primal point,
ancestors perceived a sacredness
as the uncanny look of stars in space.
New theories of origin sacrifice
their wreathing of things in holy myth.

Light waves in outward spreading rings
when striking upon becoming things
turn roundness into linear travels—
photons as waves and particles—
creating place in the directionless
non-being before a universe.

Life's body embraced by gravity
held close against infinity
let light invent the eyes to see—
made senses against an endless night
that thought-in-feeling might inherit.

Pioneers, those men and women
wove our history in their union
with their beloveds begetting children—
yearningly learning how to *mean*.
Here lately coming to consciousness
aware/unaware of light year distance,
we sense the farthest, nearest star
as explanation of our being here—
inheritors of ancient rites,
still seeking forms that celebrate
this crisis of incarnate light.

The Immortals

Half-hidden behind the forest trees
of death these await
familiarly, thought-presences
that conceal/reveal identities—
Mother the would-be saint
who praised me only
to seduce me farther from Father
Henry the suicide sullenly
apart hovering in disappearance
still my similar brother
in remembering our father strongly
enduring muscular short in stature
terse in speaking strongly authentic
Almond our uncle who haunted
these summers, schoolteacher creaking the attic
with his detective magazines
and jar of Vaseline
sneaking his rye from behind the bathtub.
These appear all unwonted
allowing me at last a static
vision of time and the hereafter—
here in my mental hubbub
assured that all final scenes
remain unburied. Thus confronted
with time as an illusion I feel their remains
return into the spirit world
unchanged—leaving me unhealed
but comforted.

A Survivor

Like the survivor of a war
whose memories mark the place
of a bombed-out former culture
I open my manuscripts and trace
these lines on paper.

Since now I write as I please
and presently no one cares
I pen for my psychic ease
recalling old wars and despairs
now echoing what no one hears.

The humanities lost their encounter
with digital things "that matter"—
one's sex, its political practice.
Others raced to the multiplex
history what once *came after.*

So now I vary my form
and no one gives a damn—
not my long-dead distant masters
nor the teachers of forever-afters
who went learnedly to their doom

with pedagogy that would conform
they thought and relevantly remain
though they gave up words of "the great"
as applied to the works they taught—
like dying without a scream.

Now new to an old terrain
a seldom-read poet I remain
recompensed by a mental light
when scrawling way to a thought
and a line-break turns out right.

I feel only an ironic sorrow
for colleagues whose "new tomorrow"
abandoned the past in print
and now find hardly a student
who cares where literature went.

Film History

This frame-melding crushes the crèche-
like miracle stories. Madonnas
of dissolute beauty caught on nitrate
crash out of view, Carole Lombard
dropped from the skies beyond Clark Gable
Jean Harlow's early death predicted
by her high/low locution the continent-
edge unstable, Westerns' badlands
drought-stricken Directors with dictator-
power unable to keep these Red Rivers
from the dust bowl of history. John
Ford filming Jap planes from Wake Island
makes make-believe reality like reversing
the currents of time in re-winds, Hollywood's
heavenly beauty a hell for unrecognized
girls in Technicolor fashion shows inside
melodramas of black and white, every-
one's reputation as unstable as
the San Andreas fault the San
Francisco earthquake redeemed for
the American soul by Jeanette MacDonald's
soprano soaring high over the wreckage
for God and a formerly virgin sexuality
while above the white letters *Hollywood*
insecurely on a hill the prewar
biplanes of an unready America
fly always in memory with their
red and white tailfins toward Pearl
Harbor. There Burt Lancaster lean
and muscular in his khaki uniform
fires a machine gun from atop

the deserted barracks prefiguring
the eventual defeat of the Japanese
who awakened the sleeping giant with
their sneak attack, bringing on
themselves the two terrible mushroom
clouds about which no good movie
has been made. The serpent still turns
in the harbor of Oahu, the *Arizona*
bleeding up drops of oil for the tourists.
The two leis thrown upon the harbor
by Deborah Kerr and Donna Reed
(the most virginal-looking former prostitute
in American film, including Jane Fonda)
float ambiguously in memory out to sea.

King Kong with the doll-sized woman
in his fist still wonders what to do—
can't climb the twin towers of yesteryear—
so Tarzan swings in on a vine, Jane as
respectable as Esther Williams in her
one-piece Sixties swimsuit, executives
rising to fall together as Tom Cruise
laughs maniacally on the Scientology
exposé the most unbelievable film ever made.
Lionel Barrymore is not yet in his
wheelchair though wheedling and needy
in *Grand Hotel* yet has all the luck
European wars in the distance while
the U.S. in Hardy Boys isolation
despite the mobs and prostitution
clings to its exceptional identity
this self-image reflected on a silver
screen of a young nation almost

as virginal as the girls arising from
the producers couches into roles
they can play from here to eternity
the good girl the good-hearted whore
the saintly mother Bette Davis after
the sanatorium with better eyebrows
smoking one of the two cigarettes lighted
by Paul Henreid on the liner's deck
while Jimmy Stewart in Hitchcock's
Technicolor by the bay will never
recover from the falling body double
signifying Kim Novak, the marker
of the vertigo of innocence in America
where there's no longer a curtain that closes.

Mind as Metaphor

The most prominent group of words used to describe mental
events are visual. . . . These words are all metaphors and the
mind-space to which they apply is a metaphor of actual space.
    —Julian Jaynes

I

A stream below a granite ridge
seems Earth's near edge
where four boulders loom heavily out
so I feel their momentum toward sunset.
Pines now lengthen on the cliff height
crowns still rosy in a slant of light.
On the opposite bank three Christmas ferns
burn in shade with their green returns.
Rapids dash and pool into the stream
of my perceptions—an elastic time
that slows and holds the knobby face
of an ironwood upside down on the surface.
Wetness pervades in a sentience
and I imagine the leaves piled underfoot
as covering my psyche's deeper root—
this sky-roofed ravine with loamy floor
a giant earth-mind in metaphor.

II

My own interior land
takes in the landscape in small
and models from a part to the whole.
Things in this mirror correspond:
a tree held in air and on a pond.
A circle that the horizon inscribes
moves with my motion and recedes.

Feeling its light infuse the air
aware of itself as being aware
my mind thinks itself dimensionless
but projects a replica form in space
like reflections on a water-surface.
An idea like a dropping pebble
spreads its point into a circle
and ring on ring each pine as datum
expands into a forest-theorem—
my *I* behind invisibly
a clarity
wherein I see.

III

Seeing is a river through—
both rapids and the mountain's view—
my mind the plain the unchanging frame
of the constantly changing chain in time.

IV

I set out in late afternoon
with not enough light for my return.
The perception of this depth of field
extends its gift to my mind.
Pines one and another recede into distance
the air between us a clearer substance
like sky on the river surface
while this sky-dome deepens toward darkness.
An idea appears as a point—
inarticulate a firstness preceding the *late*—
like this star now piercing afternoon
a-spacial, visually alone
just the glint of idea before
thinking expands it—a sense pure
of explanation my mind a space
wherein the event of thought takes place.

V

Bright belted hunter old Orion
arising in the west horizon
spies haunches of the crouching lion.
The brilliant sapphire point of Vega
summons the dimmer strings of Lyra.
These star-light touches trailing music
wake a deeper form-harmonic.
Such recognitions "outside time"
precede like Forms in Plato's Phaedo—
I seeing the many as similar—
how each particular star
marks part of Orion's figure.
By the river this December,
among resemblances I find
reflections of my questing mind
as creator and mirror.

VI

The "once-upon" of a nursery rhyme
returns my musing to childhood time.
In this invented land of fairy tale
the years reassemble, freed from the jail
of failure, of *now too late*. Time *seems*
gathered into wholes, years the streams
flowing into this all-suspending ocean
where no event has posed its final *once*.

In this séance without lighting, pure chance
is victor, Jack above the candlestick
for as long as we wish, knowing the trick
of an unsinged landing. Time in its symmetry
goes forward and in reverse, a sky
without evening its circle unbroken.
We travel our road and the one not taken.
The mind in its waking feels equal
to all history no choice irrevocable
no mistake finally made, the balanced needle
not pointing a single direction in its fall.

VII

Downhill clearing the stream-edge
I encounter a hidden knowledge.
This Seven Mile Creek by my house
winds along the river—this nearer course
through a tangle of vines like my early life.
Honeysuckle snakes up a sapling beech
grooving the trunk with its abusive touch.
I search for one early star.

The air here seems an azure tissue
a flattened depth of translucent color.
The horizon engraves far trees upon it
as twigs now darken each moment.
Could the high aspirations in my head so bend
under the honeysuckle-tangles of heredity
and experiences encoded like entropy?

As twilight deepens, these oaks inquire
like fractal baskets reaching for a star—
like the idea of a universe-beginning
in my wooden words, seeking a meaning.
Here in obscurity suddenly turning
I find Orion. Then Vega in Lyra.
Then Jupiter white and steady
in unearthly wonder higher
and clearer. These points of thought ignite
on a fading of the usual light.

VIII

A rose-window-like collector—
this giant metal flower—
spreads petals beside the supercollider.
Here priest-like underground physicists serve
the super-rational quest that they may not give
a name to: this seeking of a final cause
whereby the universe exists. Intense
magnetism has condensed a possible evidence—
if the raying paths reveal a requisite energy
that fits the theory, if the self-imposed duty
of ultimate searching may be born, at this bourne
between partial knowledge and a final unknown.
If these in another age became servants
of the metaphysical, if then the Scholastic Savants
philosophized eternity, still the stasis
of thought they sought remains as absolute
as their Cathedral spires—as acute.

IX

In one orbital plane planets wheel
around the sun, its great sphere
of fusing hydrogen pulled to cohere
within the vast weakness of gravity, giant
in this massive generation of light.
Photons traverse the vacuum without weight
invisibly infusing a darkness
that is the default condition of space
until rays touch a refractive substance
and night is defined by its opposite.
As our eyes evolved for the light
so our neurons feel a thought-luminescence
in the presence of stars, our senses
pierced by their bright randomness
in the dance of forces that we *are*, within lips
that may speak and kiss, our little eclipse
of sleep so small in the galaxy, light's presence
extending like a consciousness through space.
Located by a down toward Earth
we feel-recall the separation by birth
from the round world without time
or gravity, when we swam a primal ocean
in a sensation we live to retrieve
as connection to the all in filial love.

Inner Landscapes

The sky curves above its horizon
in landscapes of sunlight and haze.
Rivers carve a winding division
pine needles filter sun's rays.

A brook across stones fractures light
a lake's reach is bluer in distance.
Afternoons edge against twilight
skies dapple meadows by chance

as wind-moved shadows pass over
trailed by the white billowed clouds.
A blue dome appears to hover
peopled by these far-dreaming heads.

Wild grasses frame a farm's rows.
A road and a bridge give sight
of a river's deeper repose
within the current's freshening of light.

Shingles of a house sense the stars
when a sleeper dreams it is so
as he wanders lost kingdoms holy wars
mind-divided into above and below.

A miasma of collective memories
from the plains and caves of origin
recall children thrown down to deities
in a sacrifice like original sin.

Churches' crossed steeples upraised
recall the fallen selves who believed
that a body so in darkness dazed
would by its soul's arising be saved.

The chaos we wake to escape
holds the soul in caves of memory.
Delivered to a one-life landscape,
we ignorantly explore toward eternity.

All need as companion the sun
through the winding shadows of their way—
each morning returning like one
who travels this darkness back to day.

So rays on meadowland sparkling
with the river's dashing upon stone
frames a landscape's re-imagining—
the soul-traveler no longer alone.

From a chaos of sleep he recovers
into dawn-light golden through trees—
this sun like a radiant savior's
ascent from an underworld's miseries.

Then daylight and a brighter weather
picture the psyche's new mirror—
its space a cerulean ether
and darkness only night's metaphor.

Why Space Is Time

Here in a December house
I see through spaceship windows
noticing that the Earth in thus
orbiting a star has directed
the inclination of our axis
of rotation away from the heat
felt when the golden-platinum
hole in the hemisphere of air
most blindingly flashes.

Now light has a late look a slant
already toward nightfall though in
mid-afternoon. This air is emptier
of warmer promise standing like
invisible rooms wherein leaves
dried by their time aloft slide down
the eddying gusts, crusts of
the rich bread of summer—
portending the chill when white walls
glow bluish toward nightfall—
recalling days when as children
we drank the skim milk light
hungry for the yellow butter of sun.
Alive then running we felt night
so far that the grass under our feet
could never gather dew.

Now our spaceship's journey has
left those empty rooms behind it.
There is something called a past—
meaning a place in orbits before

invisibly existing in another
dimension as a thing called
time—now casting these colorless
shadows of longing through windows
this broken look of branches.

So we feel that we are voyaging
through the emptiness of space
where hurts occurred but in orbits
ago that are not now present.
Yet somehow in this lessening
color of light toward December
a house holds plaster,
wood lath showing at broken places—
a ceiling that one day fell
in one big piece near the door
onto a woman carrying a tray
of dishes from the kitchen and broke
onto her head and we kids laughed.

Today such light is filling the room
while from my eyes a glancing
homeward flashes to the windows
where outside over the tin-roofed
houses of *then* I see two swallows
flying spelling "already evening."

So now I believe in another
dimension a space wherein there
are times and the times
held there stay present in parallel—
a house with white walls

made of one shade of afternoon
where the seasons layer on
endlessly,

solacing the ignorance
and greediness of our loves
forgiving each other's incompletions
realizing that each orbit's
once can never be enough
so that the particles that we are
hum and circulate like bees seeking
their hive returning in honey of sunlight
to the gathered days preserved
in golden combs.

A Walk in the Park

I

In a riverside park
the wooden bridge I walk
gives back to my foot
its harmonic vibration—
in tune with my step then not.
A man in love with a woman
finds her responsive passion
an answering other nature—
a mirror of inner desire—
both inside-outsides together
sharing a deep interior.

In love-making the two come home
similar and different in form
going out for a desired return
though the beginning may be uncertain.
Each bridges for the other—
vibrating sometimes in tune
like these wooden planks over water—
suspending the two in between
one bank of time and the other.

II

But in falling out of tune
the two are on their own
vibrating to random statics
of car and cell phone traffics—
each with private obsessions

not disloyal to the other
as with another lover
just being the different persons
everyone usually is
in times not joined by passion.
Love has its miseries
for persons living this series
of according ephemeral moments.

III

Now returning in my walk
I renew the chance of my step
on a wooden plank still wet
from a rain just gone
and think longingly of this woman.
As passions with age grow rarer
we both more willingly weather
each fruitful storm
so long as the vessel comes home
with man and woman as couple—
equally able to harm and to heal.

Past the nonsense violence
of sirens that lashed him to the mast
this sadder wiser Odysseus
comes home again at last
admiring how his Penelope
forgives and receives—
she the myth by which he lives.

Road Kill

The dark sisters continue their vigil.
Their hieratic presences in half light
by the busier-than-ever county road
dip ceremonially into the carcass. This death
belongs to them. No one to claim or remove
their dog-sized white tail. The horizon
flattens and draws in, the doll-house
houses with Mom and Dad and Buster
black and white silent movie frames as
real as this era-pantomime: a succession
of stop-action images without the illusion
of motion. Time snips apart into instants
that flatten against the silhouette trees,
while only the spectral birds and their meal
stay real. The small dark heads with ivory
curves of bill arise, as in conversation
or inquisition: question marks against
the honeysuckled fence. The former pasture
beyond recedes earlier and earlier until
death on the doorstep italicizes life.

Dreaming England

Winchester Cathedral's thorn work
entangles our limbs in cursives
like song become stone. Desire cuts
as hard as screens into air where over
the rolling dells our flesh scrolls out
its historic inscription, we the lives
of makers of hay in fields below us.
Covers in the Bed and Breakfast curvet
around as if carved by an ancient mason.
We'd lived amid a crucifix music
unfalling from high in air in sleep
into present sunlight, diffusing our
ardors across meadows and rye where
from oak-topped rises we bled downhill in
creases of rivulets toward the Thames.
Lovers throughout the many ages we
had devoured each other's figures
intertwining our limbs with the landscape
while waking in an English worship where
we'd returned to understand our own—
I an Abelard with testicles you
an uncloistered Eloise, our shame
only ignorance, where times had
cast us into unlettered farmlands.
Our ancestors dared across the seas
the Miss Forrest we read of at Jamestown
numbered with my people among the dead.
Now come to recover the intelligence
of words made flesh in a northern
climate, we slough off the stumps of
old time steamboat landings, at low tide

in August—Pitch Kettle Maple Apple—
the vernacular of an inhabitancy that
lost its theology in swamps and pocosins.
In England we reignite our lust for
the Word, entangling two kingdoms
in bas relief, erecting chapels and naves
anew as the landscapes of our minds
enrich themselves, we emissaries
of reunion, her families Gascoine and
Forrest mine Applethwaite and Mercer
we stitching fields together with hedgerows
threading footpaths from village to village
entrenching identity in churchyard stones.
Distantly we knew already those English
whom we met, the tweedy vested gentleman
who instructed us in slicing the scone
then spreading the clotted cream on
both these sides, with jam also. We went
happily ignorant with our kids for working
class Fish and Chips, loving the fried
cod and potatoes, wondering at the green,
almost tasteless broad beans. We stood
beside the Bristol Channel at Porlock Weir
watching the tide rush out over boulders
and football sized and cannon ball rounded
beach stones, the oceanward horizon historic
with a ship-shaped rock sailing perpetually
westward. Again when only we two together
we kept in our eyes the dells and downs
of past ages our passions ringing out
with circles of rooks at evening, we
articulate together in each other's arms.
We held each other as in past pages, in

the thorny script of monk manuscripts
that here our genes indite deeper with
children and their children. Now our
limbs overlaid as in escutcheons dream
this ancestry like a pulsing of effigies.
As an inscription articulates a thematic
line within time so our quest for love
and true knowledge in its places and contexts
has led us beyond our first horizons
in a history trip across the centuries.
So in this retrospect of aging we
inscribe our pages knowingly, recalling
the tracery of fellow crossers of the Bridge
of Angels above the clay yellow Tiber,
the echoing dome of St. Peter's shaping
our horizon toward meaning, recalling
the strata of forebears stacked genetically
like the Popes in holy layers below
the altar and cathedra in a stained-glass
knowledge of love and death throughout the ages.

So again in England laced together by
tendrils of dreaming in each other's arms
we feel sunfire lighten again in our tracery
carving carols across the woodland ridges.
Like knights and ladies in limestone we
tower among the hills of Somerset in trips
we took, pilgrims to Glastonbury, converts
to a new religion of ancientness, imprinting
our eyes with stained glass of martyrdoms
and holy births, we two small figures
down aisles together between pews
under holy stonework, beginning again

always born and begetting in many-made
centuries, our lust fire unended
while even now molded into the past
like a filigreed screen before the high altar
through which the anthems of praises echo still.

The Serpent

The stained glass fractals-in-motion
crumple farmlands, black-limbed
riverside trees the leading that borders
these glimpses. Sinuously times fold
deeper, limbs of lovers ramify in darkness
asphalt hardening the surfaces. Plates
tectonically sliding pull under
the windows of this past as the writhing
increases, memorializing family markers
caught in oily coilings. Farmyard privies
raise walls of private retrospect, churches
without space enough to letter in color
the thighs and breasts of rural unions
leave tatters of silk in mind while
pennants upheld by armies of the night
flutter a shredded mourning, families
in glass preserving lost innocence
though leaden lines enclosing them
write-erase illegibilities of loss.
Autos in lists of lanes now lancing
with headlights freeze the serpent
a moment in its coilings where
broken windowpanes look out
onto dragons of traffic, lives frail
under banners of smoke from monster
factories. Shale formations shift
convulsively in Oklahoma. Grand
Canyon ravines winding their
layered sinuosities into down-
veed vistas frame the sunset windows
of the stained glass still-moving serpent.

An End of Analysis

I

This moment as I placed it in
time surrounded her face
taking it away downstream
while I went with the great drift
back into afternoon traffic.

                    No romance
haloed her vanishing—only our evocation
of time in its curlings and hoverings.
I had projected a timeless anima
upon her, and she had freed me.

                      Under
the thunderclouds, a slant of sun knifed through.
So we vectored apart, along separate
axes of this clear unseeable drift of days.
I felt an instant nostalgia, and the possibility
of living in the moment.

                    The end of analysis
meant there was no next time on the calendar.
It was like "real life," except that "the next"
And "the next" had been erased by agreement
between us—no more that she could do for my
"backward longing"—my emotional currency
radically devalued, buying me no more of
that "anticipated time" in which we live.

II

On this late outpost this island Earth,
time is wind in through a window
bending the match flame as it picks
out a dilated pupil and catches the flicker
of an eyelid. Outside, a parking lot
festers in spring heat. Somnolent summer
in the offing brings cloud towers
with blue-black bottoms, overawing
the fallow farmlands, dappling
cemetery stones on the green slope
with transparent shadow—sweeping
July upon us and then on
into fall, adding new creases
to my forehead, printing me with
days that recur and recur, never the same.

Seeming outside us, our thoughts run
on in their round as if we were
islands swept along somehow in
this seaward flowing, except that
the ocean reservoir we imagine
at the end of our days is only
stones on a hill. Yet a conversation from
beyond the horizon seems going on still—
we all taking part in this timelessness
that our thoughts propose, unreconciled
to our single journey's dumb conclusion.

III

This unseen current swirls around
us, draining sunlight from faces
taking our bodies downstream, in
this clear invisible river where eddies
are days and falls the years, that
only we humans enumerate—
this continual going, that sweeps
the meadow and farmlands to autumn.

This element of our seeing/feeling
gives us our breath and takes it from us,
inventing birth and death. We know
only the ride in between, this age-ward
motion, from childhood's stretched-
out hours toward the beach and
the forever-droning of sermons, to
a quickening pace, making evenings
together quicker, bringing the Christmases
closer, in changes parodied by
calendars, their months and seasons.
These hours defeat expectations—sometimes
fulfilling them, bringing surprises—
a rainbow against the clouds, from a mountain
pathway—the forever sounding waves, at sea-sides—
the ocean's transient, semi-returning of us
to childhood, our castles of sand washed
over and rebuilt—like our dreams.

I remember body-surfing with our sons,
we curling with the breaking wave,
becoming part of its momentum

skimming along in the foam across
sandy gravel and the broken shells
then raising our heads from this ocean-
edge as if just arrived on the continent
of time. We'd arise dripping, go inland
through the salt white sand over the boardwalk
through the sea oat dunes to a cottage,
where we'd charcoal a fresh sea bass
on a deck overlooking the live oaks,
toward a sunset glittering the inlet.

IV

Out of the city along the freeway
in the brilliant present of sunlight
I felt the mortality of instants.
The jetliner lifting off flew into
each dangerous slice of the potential.
I felt the radical mortality of the possible,
as each infinitesimal bit of it
shattered onto the angled wings and
scattered in sunlight, into this freedom
and brilliance and loss. Thoughts flicked
onto the screen of my mind
and vanished. My eyes and hands and
arms were guiding the vehicle onto
a viaduct above the crossing traffic.
I felt myself a creature without a past.
Existential came to mind uninvited—
my loneliness powerful and dangerous.
I was trying for a moment this living
in a space between past and future—
flying beside the liner without wings.

V

An acute solitary remembrance
carrying us together across the years
was guiding me homeward, I pierced
by a sense of our continuance.

When in foreseeing wish I arrive
my wife is as she was
in those early married seasons—
our grandchildren as if the ages of their
prepubescent parents—our children.

Wishing, I feel beginnings
should middle on toward endings,
retaining the consort
that the movement's all about—
not that brutal stop
dismissing the audience.

So vividly I imagine,
suddenly it all seems real—

pasts and futures together
parts of that single picture
we dream from and believe—
our ends and beginnings
joining as in our longings,
for that sonata form we give
this music of being alive.

I grieve that this wish
lives only in our minds, not part
of these sequences—this flesh's
loves in time—only an art,
of our fanatically believing hearts.

www.ingramcontent.com/pod-product-compliance
Lightning Source LLC
Chambersburg PA
CBHW022150090426
42742CB00010B/1460